THE BOOK OF
FIVE RINGS

from SmarterComics

MIYAMOTO MUSASHI

THE BOOK OF
FIVE RINGS

from SmarterComics

MIYAMOTO MUSASHI

Mark Dos Santos	Pencils & Ink
Tony Fleecs	Production Manager Colors & Letters
Lauren Perry	Color Separations
Cullen Bunn	Script
D.J. Kirkbride	Editor
Jennifer Kunz	Creative Director
Sander Pieterse	Media Designer
Franco Arda	CEO SmarterComics

Special Thanks to Chris Moreno & Tone Rodriguez

ISBN-13: 978-1-61082-001-1

Copyright © 2011 SmarterComics, LLC.

Printed in Canada

FOREWORD

Earth. Water. Fire. Wind. Void.

These are the elements – the essential building blocks – of a style of a nearly unbeatable philosophy of swordsmanship.

The samurai is now an iconic figure in pop culture. From books to movies and television, from video games to–yes–comic books; the samurai warrior paints a picture in our minds of unparalleled discipline and combat prowess. Although the samurai only constituted roughly ten percent of their society, they cast a long shadow. Many men and women still practice the way of the samurai today.

Miyamoto Musashi was one of the greatest samurai in history. At the age of 13, he fought his first opponent. He fought in sixty life–or–death matches over the course of his life, and he never lost. He was a master of swordsmanship, strategy, and tactics and he documented his philosophy on battle – and on life – in "The Book of Five Rings."

For Miyamoto Musashi, combat and life were one and the same. In his sixty battles, he faced single opponents as well as groups of enemies intent on killing him. Like Musashi, these foes were well–trained and they wielded some of the finest instruments of death ever forged. These battles left men maimed and – more often than not – dead. One false move could mean the end of the battle and the end of your life. For a man to survive sixty opponents – each intent on killing him – he had to be more than strong… more than skilled with the sword. In cases like this, one wrong move could mean the end of your life. To survive, a warrior needed to be more than strong… more than fast   and more than skilled with a blade. He needed a code – a philosophical way – to guide him in all aspects of combat (and by extension all aspects of life).

This is the philosophy documented in "The Book of Five Rings."

The world has changed greatly since Musashi's time, but his philosophies can still be applied to day–to–day life. This is not merely a book about combat. It is a book through which combat can teach one how to truly live. Those who internalize and practice the concepts presented here will know no limits, no boundaries.

With illustrated examples of how to use the warrior philosophy in today's world, the SmarterComics version will help you wield the samurai warrior philosophy like the finest swords of old in the greatest battle of all: modern life!

Why is the samurai philosophy so relevant to today? For a samurai, a battle was a test of life or death.

For readers today, this is a winner–takes–all world.

Cullen Bunn

Earth. Water. Fire. Wind. Void.

INTRODUCTION

I HAVE SPENT MANY YEARS TRAINING IN THE *WAY OF STRATEGY.*

NOW, AS I CLIMB THIS MOUNTAIN AND KNEEL BEFORE BUDDHA, I WILL EXPLAIN THE WAY OF STRATEGY IN WRITING.

FROM YOUTH, MY HEART HAS BEEN INCLINED TOWARD THE WAY OF STRATEGY.

MY FIRST DUEL WAS WHEN I WAS THIRTEEN YEARS OLD.

I STRUCK DOWN A STRATEGIST FROM THE SHINTO SCHOOL.

WHEN I WAS SIXTEEN, I STRUCK DOWN ANOTHER ABLE STRATEGIST.

WHEN I WAS TWENTY-ONE, I WENT TO THE CAPITAL AND MET ALL MANNER OF STRATEGISTS, NEVER ONCE FAILING TO WIN MANY CONTESTS.

AFTER THAT, I WENT FROM PROVINCE TO PROVINCE, DUELING MANY STRATEGISTS OF VARIOUS SCHOOLS.

EVEN THOUGH I HAD AS MANY AS SIXTY ENCOUNTERS, I NEVER FAILED.

WHEN I REACHED THIRTY, I LOOKED BACK ON MY PAST.

THE PREVIOUS VICTORIES WERE NOT DUE TO MY HAVING MASTERED STRATEGY.

PERHAPS IT WAS NATURAL ABILITY, OR THE ORDER OF HEAVEN...

...OR THAT THE OTHER STRATEGISTS WERE SIMPLY INFERIOR.

AFTER THAT, I STUDIED MORNING AND EVENING, SEARCHING FOR THE PRINCIPLE, AND CAME TO REALIZE THE WAY OF STRATEGY WHEN I WAS FIFTY.

SINCE THEN I HAVE LIVED WITHOUT FOLLOWING ANY PARTICULAR WAY.

THUS, WITH THE VIRTUE OF STRATEGY, I PRACTICE MANY MARTIAL ARTS AND ABILITIES -- ALL WITH NO TEACHER.

TO WRITE THIS BOOK, I DID NOT USE THE LAW OF BUDDHA OR THE TEACHINGS OF CONFUCIUS.

I UTILIZED NEITHER OLD WAR CHRONICLES NOR BOOKS ON MARTIAL TACTICS.

I TAKE UP MY BRUSH AND EXPLAIN THE *TRUE SPIRIT* OF THE WAY OF STRATEGY.

THE GROUND BOOK

STRATEGY IS THE CRAFT OF THE **WARRIOR**.

COMMANDERS MUST ENACT THE CRAFT, AND THEIR TROOPS SHOULD KNOW THE WAY.

IT IS SAID THE WARRIOR'S WAY IS TWOFOLD: OF THE PEN **AND** OF THE SWORD.

EVEN IF A MAN HAS NO NATURAL ABILITY, HE CAN BE A WARRIOR BY STICKING TO BOTH DIVISIONS OF THE WAY.

GENERALLY SPEAKING, THE WAY OF THE WARRIOR IS RESOLUTE ACCEPTANCE OF DEATH.

THE WARRIOR IS DIFFERENT IN THAT STUDYING THE WAY OF STRATEGY IS BASED ON OVERCOMING ENEMIES.

BY VICTORY GAINED IN CROSSING SWORDS WITH INDIVIDUALS, OR ENJOYING BATTLE WITH LARGE NUMBERS, WE CAN ATTAIN POWER AND FAME.

THIS IS THE VIRTUE OF **STRATEGY**.

IN OLDEN TIMES, STRATEGY WAS SEEN AS AN ART, AND IT WAS NOT LIMITED TO SWORD FENCING.

THERE ARE FOUR WAYS IN WHICH MEN PASS THROUGH LIFE...

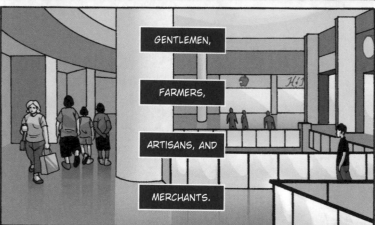

GENTLEMEN,

FARMERS,

ARTISANS, AND

MERCHANTS.

THE WAY OF THE *FARMER*.

USING AGRICULTURAL INSTRUMENTS, HE SEES SPRING THROUGH TO AUTUMN WITH AN EYE ON THE CHANGES OF SEASONS.

THE SECOND WAY IS THE WAY OF THE *MERCHANT*.

THE WAY OF THE MERCHANT IS TO LIVE BY TAKING PROFIT.

THE THIRD IS THE WAY OF THE *GENTLEMAN WARRIOR*, WHO CARRIES THE APPROPRIATE WEAPONRY.

IF A GENTLEMAN DISLIKES STRATEGY, HE WILL NOT APPRECIATE THE BENEFIT OF WEAPONRY, SO HE MUST HAVE A TASTE FOR THIS.

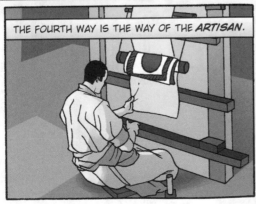

THE FOURTH WAY IS THE WAY OF THE *ARTISAN*.

THIS IS THE WAY OF THE *CARPENTER*.

THE WAY OF THE CARPENTER IS TO BECOME PROFICIENT IN THE USE OF TOOLS, FIRST TO LAY HIS PLANS WITH A TRUE MEASURE AND THEN TO PERFORM HIS WORK ACCORDINGLY.

THE COMPARISON OF STRATEGY AND CARPENTRY IS SEEN THROUGH THEIR CONNECTION IN THE BUILDING OF *HOUSES.*

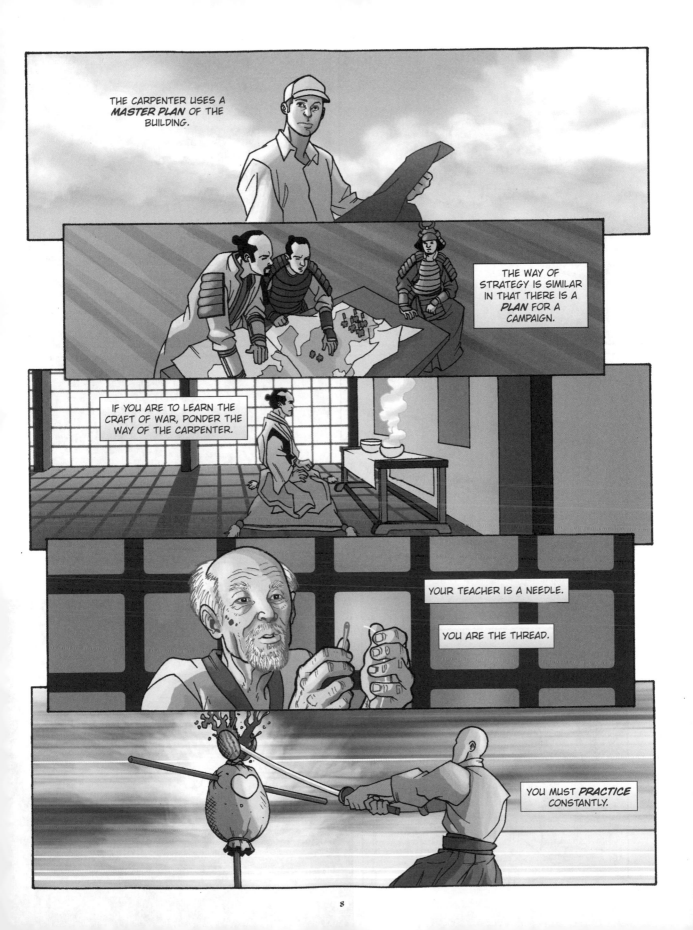

LIKE THE FOREMAN CARPENTER, THE COMMANDER MUST KNOW *NATURAL RULES*...

...AND THE RULES OF THE *COUNTRY*...

...AND THE RULES OF *HOUSES*.

IN THE CONSTRUCTION OF HOUSES, WOOD IS CHOSEN.

STRAIGHT, UN-KNOTTED TIMBER OF GOOD APPEARANCE IS USED FOR REVEALED PILLARS.

STRAIGHT TIMBER WITH SMALL DEFECTS IS USED FOR INNER PILLARS.

TIMBER OF THE FINEST APPEARANCE, EVEN IF A LITTLE WEAK, IS USED FOR THE THRESHOLDS, DOORS, AND SLIDING DOORS.

GOOD, STRONG TIMBER, EVEN IF IT IS GNARLED AND KNOTTED, CAN ALWAYS BE USED DISCREETLY IN CONSTRUCTION.

A COMMANDER MUST MAKE SIMILAR CHOICES.

STRAIGHT, UN-KNOTTED TIMBER OF GOOD APPEARANCE IS USED FOR REVEALED PILLARS.

STRAIGHT TIMBER WITH SMALL DEFECTS IS USED FOR INNER PILLARS.

TIMBER OF THE FINEST APPEARANCE, EVEN IF A LITTLE WEAK, IS USED FOR THE THRESHOLDS, DOORS, AND SLIDING DOORS.

GOOD, STRONG TIMBER, EVEN IF IT IS GNARLED AND KNOTTED, CAN ALWAYS BE USED DISCREETLY IN CONSTRUCTION.

THE FOREMAN CARPENTER ALLOTS EACH OF HIS MEN ACCORDING TO HIS ABILITY...

...FLOOR LAYERS...

...MAKERS OF SLIDING DOORS...

...MAKERS OF CEILINGS...

...AND SO ON.

IF THE FOREMAN KNOWS AND DEPLOYS HIS MEN WELL, THE FINISHED WORK WILL BE GOOD.

IT IS THE SAME WITH A COMMANDER.

...FLOOR LAYERS...

...MAKERS OF SLIDING DOORS...

...MAKERS OF CEILINGS...

...AND SO ON.

IF THE FOREMAN KNOWS AND DEPLOYS HIS MEN WELL, THE FINISHED WORK WILL BE GOOD.

THE FOREMAN MUST TAKE INTO ACCOUNT THE ABILITIES AND LIMITATIONS OF HIS MEN, CIRCULATING AMONG THEM AND ASKING NOTHING UNREASONABLE.

HE SHOULD KNOW THEIR MORALE AND SPIRIT, AND ENCOURAGE THEM WHEN NECESSARY.

STRATEGY HOLDS TO THE SAME PRINCIPLE.

THE FOREMAN MUST TAKE INTO ACCOUNT THE ABILITIES AND LIMITATIONS OF HIS MEN, CIRCULATING AMONG THEM AND ASKING NOTHING UNREASONABLE.

HE SHOULD KNOW THEIR MORALE AND SPIRIT, AND ENCOURAGE THEM WHEN NECESSARY.

LIKE A TROOPER, THE CARPENTER SHARPENS HIS OWN TOOLS.

HE CARRIES HIS EQUIPMENT IN HIS TOOL BOX AND WORKS UNDER THE DIRECTION OF HIS FOREMAN.

THIS IS THE CRAFT OF CARPENTERS.

WHEN THE CARPENTER BECOMES SKILLED AND UNDERSTANDS MEASURES, HE CAN BECOME A FOREMAN.

TO SUCCEED, THE CARPENTER MUST MAKE SURE HIS WORK IS NOT WARPED...

...THAT THE JOINTS ARE NOT MISALIGNED...

...AND THAT THE WORK IS TRULY PLANED SO THAT IT MEETS WELL AND IS NOT MERELY FINISHED.

THIS IS BUT THE FIRST OF FIVE BOOKS CONCERNING THE DIFFERENT ASPECTS OF THE WAY.

THE OTHERS INCLUDE THE *WATER* BOOK.

WITH WATER AS THE BASIS, THE SPIRIT BECOMES LIQUID.

WATER ADOPTS THE SHAPE OF ITS RECEPTACLE.

IT IS SOMETIMES A TRICKLE...

...AND SOMETIMES A MIGHTY SEA.

WHEN YOU DEFEAT ONE MAN IN COMBAT, YOU DEFEAT ANY MAN IN THE WORLD.

THE SPIRIT OF DEFEATING ONE MAN IS THE SAME FOR DEFEATING TEN MILLION MEN.

THE STRATEGIST MAKES SMALL THINGS INTO BIG THINGS, LIKE BUILDING A GREAT BUDDHA FROM A ONE FOOT MODEL.

THE PRINCIPLE OF STRATEGY IS HAVING ONE THING...

JOLENE'S
FRESH-BAKED COOKIES, INC.

...AND TO KNOW TEN THOUSAND THINGS.

Jolene's

FRESH BAKED COOK

THE THIRD BOOK IS *FIRE*.

THIS BOOK IS ABOUT *FIGHTING*.

THE SPIRIT OF FIRE IS FIERCE, WHETHER IT IS SMALL OR BIG, AND SO IT IS WITH BATTLES.

THE WAY OF BATTLES IS THE SAME FOR MAN-TO-MAN FIGHTS...

...AND FOR TEN THOUSAND A SIDE BATTLES.

YOU MUST APPRECIATE THAT SPIRIT CAN BECOME BIG OR SMALL.

WHAT IS BIG IS EASY TO PERCEIVE.

WHAT IS SMALL IS DIFFICULT TO PERCEIVE.

IT IS DIFFICULT FOR LARGE NUMBERS OF PEOPLE TO CHANGE POSITION, SO THEIR MOVEMENTS CAN BE EASILY PREDICTED.

AN INDIVIDUAL CAN EASILY CHANGE HIS MIND, SO HIS MOVEMENTS ARE DIFFICULT TO PREDICT.

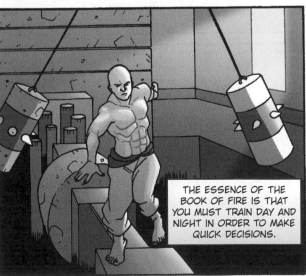

THE ESSENCE OF THE BOOK OF FIRE IS THAT YOU MUST TRAIN DAY AND NIGHT IN ORDER TO MAKE QUICK DECISIONS.

WIND IS THE FOURTH BOOK.

WIND REPRESENTS OLD TRADITIONS, PRESENT-DAY TRADITIONS, AND FAMILY TRADITIONS OF STRATEGY.

IT IS DIFFICULT TO KNOW YOURSELF IF YOU DO NOT KNOW OTHERS.

THUS, IN THE BOOK OF WIND I HAVE WRITTEN ABOUT OTHER TRADITIONS AND STRATEGIES.

FINALLY, THERE IS THE BOOK OF THE *VOID*.

BY VOID, I MEAN THAT WHICH HAS NO BEGINNING AND NO END.

ATTAINING THIS PRINCIPLE MEANS NOT ATTAINING THIS PRINCIPLE.

THE WAY OF STRATEGY IS THE WAY OF *NATURE*.

WHEN YOU APPRECIATE THE POWER OF NATURE, KNOWING THE RHYTHM OF ANY SITUATION, YOU WILL BE ABLE TO STRIKE NATURALLY.

BEFORE WE EXPLORE THE OTHER BOOKS, IT IS IMPORTANT TO KNOW THAT WARRIORS CARRY TWO SWORDS.

WARRIORS SHOULD TRAIN FROM THE START WITH THE SHORT SWORD AND LONG SWORD IN EITHER HAND.

IF YOU ARE TO SACRIFICE YOUR LIFE, YOU MUST MAKE THE FULLEST USE OF YOUR WEAPONRY.

IT IS A TRAGEDY TO DIE WITH A WEAPON YET UNDRAWN.

IF YOU HOLD A SWORD WITH BOTH HANDS, IT IS DIFFICULT TO FREELY WIELD IT FROM LEFT TO RIGHT.

MY METHOD IS TO HOLD A SWORD IN ONE HAND.

ALWAYS REMEMBER, THOUGH...

IF IT IS DIFFICULT TO STRIKE AN ENEMY DOWN WITH ONE HAND, YOU MUST USE TWO HANDS.

IT IS NOT DIFFICULT TO LEARN TO USE A SWORD WITH ONE HAND.

THE WAY TO DO THIS IS TO PRACTICE WITH TWO LONG SWORDS, ONE IN EACH HAND.

IT WILL SEEM DIFFICULT AT FIRST, BUT EVERYTHING IS DIFFICULT AT FIRST.

AS YOU BECOME ACCUSTOMED TO THE BOW, FOR EXAMPLE, YOUR PULL BECOMES STRONGER.

AS YOU BECOME USED TO WIELDING THE LONG SWORD...

... YOU WILL GAIN THE POWER OF THE WAY AND WIELD THE SWORD WELL.

YOU CAN WIN WITH A LONG WEAPON...

...AND YET YOU CAN ALSO WIN WITH A SHORT WEAPON.

IN SHORT, THE WAY IS THE SPIRIT OF *WINNING*, WHATEVER THE WEAPON.

THERE IS A TIME AND PLACE FOR USE OF WEAPONS.

THE BEST USE OF THE COMPANION SWORD IS IN A CONFINED SPACE OR WHEN YOU ARE ENGAGED CLOSELY WITH AN OPPONENT.

WITH THE SPEAR, YOU CAN TAKE THE INITIATIVE.

A HALBERD IS A DEFENSIVE WEAPON.

FROM INSIDE FORTIFICATIONS, THE GUN HAS NO EQUAL AMONG WEAPONS...

... BUT ONCE SWORDS ARE CROSSED, THE GUN BECOMES USELESS.

THERE IS TIMING IN *EVERYTHING.*

TIMING IS IMPORTANT IN DANCING AND MUSIC.

TIMING IS ALSO INVOLVED IN MILITARY ARTS.

IN ALL SKILLS AND ABILITIES, THERE IS TIMING.

THERE IS TIMING IN THE WHOLE LIFE OF THE WARRIOR.

TIMING IS IN HIS THRIVING AND HARMONY...

... AS WELL AS IN HIS DECLINE AND DISCORD.

SIMILARLY, THERE IS TIMING IN THE WAY OF THE MERCHANT, IN THE RISE AND FALL OF CAPITAL.

STOCK MARKET INDEX

IN STRATEGY, THERE ARE VARIOUS TIMING CONSIDERATIONS.

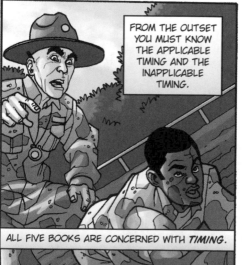

FROM THE OUTSET YOU MUST KNOW THE APPLICABLE TIMING AND THE INAPPLICABLE TIMING.

ALL FIVE BOOKS ARE CONCERNED WITH *TIMING*.

IF YOU PRACTICE DAY AND NIGHT, YOUR SPIRIT WILL NATURALLY BROADEN.

THIS IS THE WAY FOR THOSE WHO WANT TO LEARN MY STRATEGY.

DO NOT THINK DISHONESTLY.

THE WAY IS IN *TRAINING*.

BECOME ACQUAINTED WITH EVERY ART.

KNOW THE WAYS OF ALL PROFESSIONS.

DISTINGUISH BETWEEN
GAIN AND LOSS IN
WORLDLY MATTERS.

DEVELOP INTUITIVE JUDGMENT
AND UNDERSTANDING FOR
EVERYTHING.

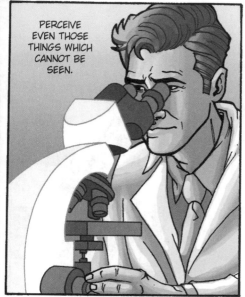

PERCEIVE
EVEN THOSE
THINGS WHICH
CANNOT BE
SEEN.

PAY ATTENTION
EVEN TO TRIFLES.

DO NOTHING WHICH IS OF NO USE.

DO NOT LET YOUR ENEMY SEE YOUR SPIRIT.

YOU MUST CULTIVATE YOUR WISDOM AND SPIRIT.

POLISH YOUR WISDOM.

LEARN PUBLIC JUSTICE.

DISTINGUISH BETWEEN GOOD AND EVIL.

$7,500

WHEN YOU CANNOT BE DECEIVED BY MEN, YOU WILL HAVE REALIZED THE WISDOM OF STRATEGY.

USED

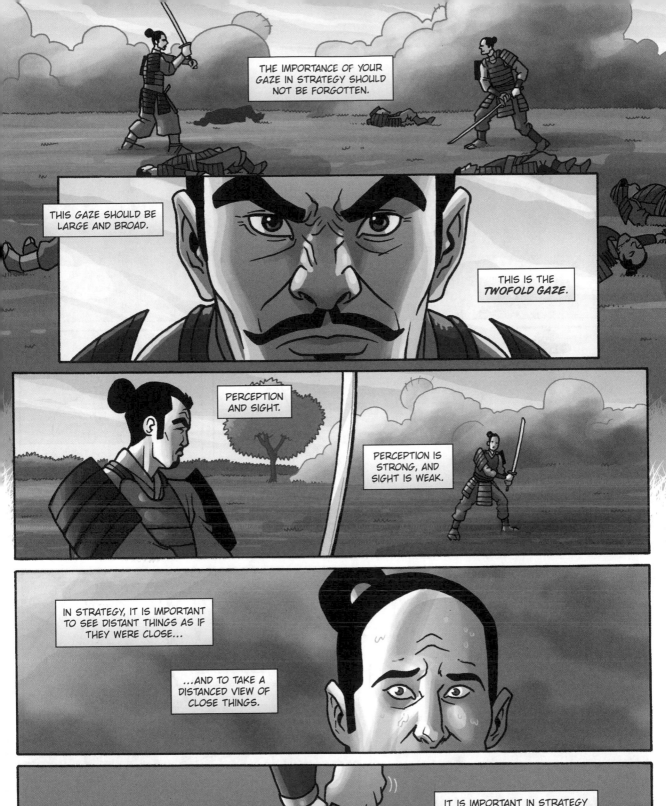

WHEN YOU TAKE UP A SWORD, YOU MUST DO SO WITH FULL INTENTION ON CUTTING THE ENEMY.

THE GRIP FOR COMBAT AND FOR SWORD-TESTING IS THE SAME.

THERE IS NO SUCH THING AS A "MAN-CUTTING" GRIP.

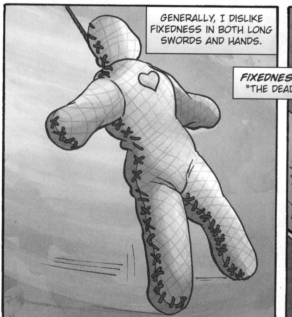

GENERALLY, I DISLIKE FIXEDNESS IN BOTH LONG SWORDS AND HANDS.

FIXEDNESS MEANS "THE DEAD HAND."

PLIABILITY EQUALS A "LIVING HAND."

WHETHER YOU MOVE FAST OR SLOW, WITH LARGE OR SMALL STEPS, YOUR FEET MUST ALWAYS MOVE AS IN NORMAL WALKING.

I DISLIKE THREE PARTICULAR WALKING METHODS...

JUMPING-FOOT, AS IT ENCOURAGES A JUMPY, INDECISIVE SPIRIT.

AND FIXED-STEP, WHICH ENCOURAGES WAITING.

FLOATING-FOOT, WHICH DISCOURAGES A FIRM STANCE.

38

KNOWING THE WAY OF THE LONG SWORD MEANS YOU CAN WIELD WITH TWO FINGERS THE SWORD THAT YOU USUALLY CARRY.

IF YOU TRY TO WIELD THE LONG SWORD QUICKLY, YOU WILL MISTAKE THE WAY.

TO WIELD THE LONG SWORD WELL YOU MUST WIELD IT *CALMLY.*

THIS IS IN LIFE AS IT IS ON THE BATTLEFIELD.

"KNOWING THE WAY OF THE LONG SWORD MEANS YOU CAN WIELD WITH TWO FINGERS THE SWORD THAT YOU USUALLY CARRY."

"IF YOU TRY TO WIELD THE LONG SWORD QUICKLY, YOU WILL MISTAKE THE WAY."

"TO WIELD THE LONG SWORD WELL YOU MUST WIELD IT *CALMLY.*"

THE FIRE BOOK

火災帳

PEOPLE THINK NARROWLY ABOUT THE BENEFIT OF STRATEGY.

IN MY STRATEGY, THE TRAINING FOR KILLING ENEMIES IS BY WAY OF MANY CONTESTS...

...FIGHTING FOR SURVIVAL...

...DISCOVERING THE MEANING OF LIFE AND DEATH...

EXAMINE YOUR ENVIRONMENT.

STAND IN THE SUN. THAT IS, TAKE UP AN ATTITUDE WITH THE SUN BEHIND YOU.

AT NIGHT, IF THE ENEMY CAN BE SEEN, KEEP THE FIRE BEHIND YOU.

YOU MUST LOOK DOWN ON THE ENEMY FROM SLIGHTLY HIGHER PLACES.

WHEN THE FIGHT COMES, CHASE THE ENEMY TOWARD AWKWARD PLACES.

ALWAYS CHASE THE ENEMY INTO BAD FOOTHOLDS, USING THE VIRTUES OF THE PLACE TO ESTABLISH PREDOMINANT POSITIONS FROM WHICH TO FIGHT.

EXAMINE YOUR ENVIRONMENT.

STAND IN THE SUN. THAT IS, TAKE UP AN ATTITUDE WITH THE SUN BEHIND YOU.

AT NIGHT, IF THE ENEMY CAN BE SEEN, KEEP THE FIRE BEHIND YOU.

YOU MUST LOOK DOWN ON THE ENEMY FROM SLIGHTLY HIGHER PLACES.

WHEN THE FIGHT COMES, CHASE THE ENEMY TOWARD AWKWARD PLACES.

ALWAYS CHASE THE ENEMY INTO BAD FOOTHOLDS, USING THE VIRTUES OF THE PLACE TO ESTABLISH PREDOMINANT POSITIONS FROM WHICH TO FIGHT.

THE FIRST METHOD.

WHEN YOU DECIDE TO ATTACK, EITHER KEEP CALM AND DASH IN QUICKLY...

...OR YOU CAN ADVANCE SEEMINGLY STRONGLY BUT WITH RESERVED SPIRIT.

ALTERNATELY, ADVANCE WITH AS STRONG A SPIRIT AS POSSIBLE...

...AND WHEN YOU REACH THE ENEMY, MOVE WITH YOUR FEET A LITTLE QUICKER THAN NORMAL, UNSETTLING AND OVERWHELMING HIM.

THE SECOND METHOD.

WHEN THE ENEMY ATTACKS, REMAIN *UNDISTURBED* -- BUT *FEIGN WEAKNESS*.

AS THE ENEMY REACHES YOU, MOVE AWAY SUDDENLY TO INDICATE THAT YOU INTEND TO JUMP ASIDE...

...THEN, ONCE THE ENEMY RELAXES -- *DASH IN!* ATTACK AS STRONGLY AS POSSIBLE.

THE THIRD METHOD.

WHEN THE ENEMY MAKES A QUICK ATTACK, YOU MUST ATTACK STRONGLY AND CALMLY.

AIM FOR HIS WEAK POINT AS YOU DRAW HIM NEAR.

ATTACK WITH ALL YOUR MIGHT, AND YOU *WILL* DEFEAT HIM.

THERE ARE OTHER METHODS FOR DEFEATING AN ENEMY THAT YOU SHOULD KNOW.

"TO HOLD DOWN A PILLOW."

IT IS BAD TO BE LED ABOUT BY THE ENEMY. MAKE THE ENEMY FOLLOW *YOU*.

IN STRATEGY, YOU MUST STOP THE ENEMY AS HE ATTEMPTS TO CUT.

YOU MUST PUSH DOWN HIS THRUST AND THROW OFF HIS HOLD WHEN HE TRIES TO GRAPPLE.

THE IMPORTANT THING IN STRATEGY IS TO SUPPRESS THE ENEMY'S *USEFUL* ACTIONS WHILE ALLOWING HIS *USELESS* ONES.

"CROSSING AT A FORD."

"CROSSING AT A FORD" MEANS, FOR EXAMPLE, CROSSING THE SEA AT A STRAIT.

I BELIEVE THIS OCCURS OFTEN IN ONE'S LIFETIME.

IT MEANS SETTING SAIL EVEN THOUGH YOUR FRIENDS STAY IN HARBOR, KNOWING THE ROUTE, KNOWING THE SOUNDNESS OF YOUR SHIP AND THE FAVOR OF THE DAY.

POWER HOUSE PUBLIC RELATIONS

WHEN ALL THE CONDITIONS ARE MET, AND THERE'S PERHAPS A FAVORABLE WIND, SET SAIL.

IF THE WIND CHANGES WITHIN A FEW MILES OF YOUR DESTINATION, YOU MUST ROLL ACROSS THE REMAINING DISTANCE WITHOUT SAIL.

IN STRATEGY, YOU MUST DISCERN THE ENEMY'S CAPABILITY AND, KNOWING YOUR OWN STRONG POINTS, "CROSS THE FORD" AT THE MOST ADVANTAGEOUS PLACE.

EVERGREEN CROSSING

1606

PR SOLUTIONS

Se

"TO KNOW THE TIMES."

"TO KNOW THE TIMES" MEANS TO KNOW THE ENEMY'S DISPOSITION IN BATTLE.

BY OBSERVING THE SPIRIT OF THE ENEMY'S MEN AND GETTING THE BEST POSITION, YOU CAN WORK OUT THE ENEMY'S DISPOSITION AND MOVE YOUR MEN ACCORDINGLY.

"TO TREAD DOWN THE SWORD."

THIS PRINCIPLE IS OFTEN USED IN STRATEGY.

WHEN THE ENEMY ATTACKS FIRST, DISCHARGING BOWS AND GUNS, IT IS DIFFICULT FOR US TO RETALIATE IF WE ARE BUSY LOADING POWDER INTO OUR OWN GUNS AND ARROWS FOR OUR BOWS.

THE SPIRIT IS TO ATTACK QUICKLY WHILE THE ENEMY IS STILL SHOOTING WITH BOWS OR GUNS.

THE SPIRIT IS TO WIN BY "TREADING DOWN" AS WE RECEIVE THE ENEMY'S ATTACK.

"TO KNOW *COLLAPSE*."

EVERYTHING CAN COLLAPSE.

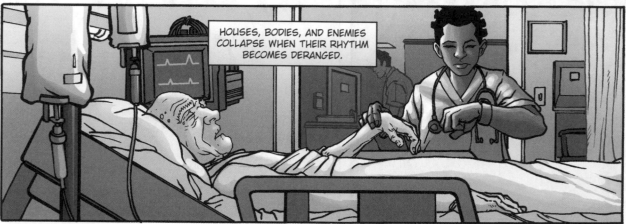

HOUSES, BODIES, AND ENEMIES COLLAPSE WHEN THEIR RHYTHM BECOMES DERANGED.

WHEN THE ENEMY STARTS TO COLLAPSE YOU MUST PURSUE HIM WITHOUT LETTING THE CHANCE GO.

IF YOU FAIL TO TAKE ADVANTAGE OF YOUR ENEMY'S COLLAPSE, HE MAY RECOVER.

"TO BECOME THE ENEMY."

THINK YOURSELF INTO THE ENEMY'S POSITION.

PEOPLE TEND TO FEAR THE ENEMY IS STRONG, AND SO THEY BECOME CAUTIOUS.

BUT IF YOU HAVE GOOD SOLDIERS, UNDERSTAND THE PRINCIPLES OF STRATEGY, AND KNOW HOW TO *BECOME* THE ENEMY, THERE IS NO CAUSE FOR WORRY.

"TO MOVE THE SHADE."

WHEN YOU CANNOT SEE THE ENEMY'S POSITION, INDICATE THAT YOU ARE ABOUT TO ATTACK STRONGLY TO DISCOVER HIS RESOURCES.

THIS MAY REQUIRE A BLUFF OR A FEINT, BUT THE ENEMY WILL SHOW HIS INTENTIONS.

"TO PASS ON."

MANY THINGS ARE SAID TO BE PASSED ON.

SLEEPINESS CAN BE PASSED ON, AS CAN YAWNING.

WHEN THE ENEMY IS AGITATED AND AND SUCCUMB TO THE INCLINATION TO RUSH, DO NOT MIND IN THE LEAST.

ROMEO AND JULIET

MAKE A SHOW OF COMPLETE CALMNESS, AND THE ENEMY WILL BE TAKEN BY THIS, BECOMING RELAXED.

WHEN YOU SEE THAT THIS SPIRIT HAS BEEN PASSED ON, YOU CAN BRING ABOUT THE ENEMY'S DEFEAT BY ATTACKING STRONGLY.

YOU WIN BY RELAXING YOUR BODY AND SPIRIT AND THEN, CATCHING ON THE MOMENT THE ENEMY RELAXES, ATTACKING STRONGLY AND QUICKLY.

THE WIND BOOK

WITHOUT KNOWLEDGE OF THE WAYS OF OTHER SCHOOLS, IT IS DIFFICULT TO UNDERSTAND THE ESSENCE OF *MY* SCHOOL.

LOOKING AT OTHER SCHOOLS, WE FIND SOME THAT SPECIALIZE IN THE TECHNIQUES OF STRENGTH USING EXTRA-LONG SWORDS.

SOME SCHOOLS STUDY THE SHORT SWORD.

SOME SCHOOLS TEACH DEXTERITY IN LARGE NUMBERS OF SWORD TECHNIQUES.

SOME SCHOOLS HAVE A LIKING FOR *ONLY* EXTRA-LONG SWORDS.

FROM THE POINT OF VIEW OF MY STRATEGY, THESE MUST BE SEEN AS WEAK SCHOOLS...

...BECAUSE THEY DO NOT APPRECIATE THE PRINCIPLE OF CUTTING THE ENEMY BY ANY MEANS.

SOME SCHOOLS FOCUS ON USING STRENGTH TO OVERPOWER AN ENEMY.

BUT YOU SHOULD NOT SPEAK OF STRONG AND WEAK SWORDS.

IF YOU JUST WIELD THE LONG SWORD IN A STRONG SPIRIT, YOUR CUTTING WILL BECOME COARSE, AND IF YOU USE THE SWORD COARSELY, YOU WILL HAVE DIFFICULTY WINNING.

IF YOU ARE ONLY CONCERNED WITH THE STRENGTH OF YOUR SWORD, YOU WILL TRY TO CUT UNREASONABLY STRONGLY...

...AND WILL NOT BE ABLE TO CUT AT ALL.

WHEN YOU CROSS SWORDS WITH AN ENEMY, DO YOU NOT THINK OF CUTTING HIM EITHER STRONGLY OR WEAKLY.

JUST THINK OF *CUTTING* AND *DEFEATING* HIM.

IF YOU RELY SOLELY ON STRENGTH WHEN YOU HIT THE ENEMY'S SWORD, YOU WILL INEVITABLY HIT TOO HARD.

IF YOU DO THIS, YOUR OWN SWORD WILL BE CARRIED ALONG AS A RESULT.

IF YOU HAVE A STRONG ARMY AND ARE RELYING ON STRENGTH TO WIN, BUT THE ENEMY ALSO HAS A STRONG ARMY, THE FIGHT WILL BE *FIERCE*.

WITHOUT THE CORRECT PRINCIPLE, THEN, THE FIGHT CANNOT BE WON.

SOME SCHOOLS FOCUS ON THE USE OF THE SHORT SWORD IN BATTLE.

SOME MEN USE SHORTER SWORDS WITH THE INTENTION OF JUMPING IN AND STABBING THE ENEMY AT THE UNGUARDED MOMENT WHEN HE FLOURISHES HIS SWORD.

BUT THIS IS A COMPLETELY DEFENSIVE MANEUVER.

THE SURE WAY TO WIN IS BY *CONTROLLING* THE BATTLE.

SOME SCHOOLS TEACH *VARIOUS* METHODS OF USING THE LONG SWORD IN ORDER TO GAIN THE ADMIRATION OF BEGINNERS.

PLATINUM GYM

TO DELIBERATE OVER MANY WAYS OF CUTTING DOWN A MAN IS IN ERROR.

CUTTING DOWN THE ENEMY IS THE WAY OF STRATEGY, AND THERE IS NO NEED FOR MANY REFINEMENTS.

KICKBOXING CLASSES

FREE WEI

KUNG FU

KRAV MAGA

LATIN DA

Yoga

SOME SCHOOLS MAINTAIN THAT THE EYES SHOULD BE FIXED ON THE ENEMY'S LONG SWORD.

SOME SCHOOLS FIX THE EYES ON THE HANDS.

SOME FIX EYES ON THE FACE, AND SO ON.

IF YOU FIX THE EYES ON THESE PLACES YOU WILL BECOME CONFUSED, YOUR STRATEGY *THWARTED*.

WHEN YOU BECOME ACCUSTOMED TO SOMETHING, YOU ARE NOT LIMITED TO THE USE OF YOUR EYES..

WHEN YOU HAVE FOUGHT MANY TIMES, YOU WILL EASILY BE ABLE TO APPRAISE THE SPEED AND POSITION OF THE ENEMY'S SWORD.

IN STRATEGY, FIXING THE EYES MEANS GAZING AT THE MAN'S HEART.

SOME SCHOOLS FOCUS ON *SPEED*.

BUT SPEED IS ESPECIALLY BAD IN THE WAY OF STRATEGY.

IF YOU TRY TO CUT QUICKLY, YOU RUN THE RISK OF MISSING YOUR TARGET IN ANY MEANINGFUL WAY WHILE ALSO EXHAUSTING YOURSELF BEFORE THE BATTLE IS OVER.

WHEN YOUR SPIRIT IS NOT IN THE LEAST CLOUDED, WHEN THE CLOUDS OF BEWILDERMENT CLEAR AWAY...

...THERE IS THE *TRUE VOID*.

IN THE VOID IS *VIRTUE*... AND NO EVIL.

WISDOM HAS EXISTENCE, PRINCIPLE HAS EXISTENCE, AND THE WAY HAS EXISTENCE.

SPIRIT IS *NOTHINGNESS*.

THE TRUE WAY OF SWORD FENCING IS THE CRAFT OF DEFEATING THE ENEMY IN A FIGHT, AND *NOTHING* OTHER THAN THIS.

IF YOU ATTAIN AND ADHERE TO THE WISDOM OF MY STRATEGY, YOU NEED NEVER DOUBT THAT YOU *WILL* WIN!

"SPEED AND STRENGTH ARE MEANINGLESS
UNLESS THEY RESULT IN VICTORY"

MIYAMOTO MUSASHI

About the Author

Infamous 17th century samurai **MIYAMOTO MUSASHI** (1584–1645) never lost a fight. His unprecedented winning streak wasn't based on supernatural powers: he was a keen master of strategy, timing, and the nuances of human interaction. He recorded his brilliant observations in „The Book of Five Rings" in 1643.

By reading only a few pages one can see immediately why books based on Musashi's life and writings have sold over 100 million copies.

About the Artists

MARK DOS SANTOS likes to draw comics.

Mark's most recent work is a comics adaptation of the horror/sci–fi classic IT! The Terror from Beyond Space for IDW. Other comics work includes Cthulu Tales and the Eureka comic based on the hit Syfy show for BOOM! Studios, Grimm Fairy Tales (Zenescope), and Johnny Repeat (Citizen Press). His illustration work includes clients like Duncan Yo–Yo, Rittenhouse Archives, and Lucasfilm.

WWW.MARKDOSSANTOS.COM

TONY FLEECS is the writer and artist of In My Lifetime, an autobiographical comic book. First published in 2006, 'Lifetime was an immediate critical success, featured twice in Wizard magazine, in the Comic Buyers guide and on the Aint–It–Cool–News.

Currently Tony is drawing an hilarious and as–yet–unannounced graphic novel for Oni Press which he co–wrote with Joshua Fialkov and writing an (also) as–yet–unannounced mini–series which will feature art by superstar artist Tone Rodriguez.

Outside of comics Tony has done illustration and design for Stan Lee's Time Jumper, 20th Century Fox, Bongo Comics, Marvel/Rittenhouse, The Milwaukee Brewers, The Cincinnati Bengals, South Dakota Tourism, The Great Lakes Loons, The Weinstein company, Monster Garage, major hospitals, insurance providers and banks.

His comics have been published by Random House (Villard), Image Comics, Silent Devil Inc., Terminal Press, IDW and Boom! Studios.

Currently Fleecs lives in Los Angeles. His mother says he is handsome.

WWW.FLEECSDESIGN.COM

Other titles from
SmarterComics™

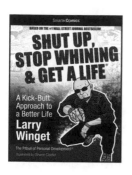

SHUT UP, STOP WHINING & GET A LIFE
from SmarterComics

by Larry Winget

Internationally renowned success philosopher, business speaker, and humorist, Larry Winget offers advice that flies in the face of conventional self–help. SHUT UP, STOP WHINING, AND GET A LIFE forces all responsibility for every aspect of your life right where it belongs: on you.

THE ART OF WAR from SmarterComics

by Sun Tzu

Written by an ancient Chinese military general and philosopher, THE ART OF WAR reveals the subtle secrets of successful competition – equally applicable to war, business, politics, sports, law, poker, gaming, and life. Required reading in modern business schools!

THE LONG TAIL from SmarterComics

by Chris Anderson

Now in comic format, this 2006 New York Times bestseller introduced the business world to a future that's already here. It explains why the focus of Internet commerce is not on hits but on misses—the long tail of the demand curve – and illuminates the reasons behind the success of niche operations like Amazon.com, iTunes, and Netflix. A must–read for every entrepreneur and manager.

OVERACHIEVEMENT from SmarterComics

by Dr. John Eliot

In OVERACHIEVEMENT from SmarterComics, Dr. Eliot offers the rest of us the unconventional and counterintuitive concepts embraced by Olympic athletes, business moguls, rock stars, top surgeons, salespeople, and financial experts who have turned to him for performance–enhancement advice.

Other titles from
SmarterComics™

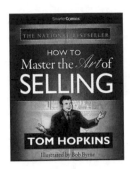

HOW TO MASTER THE ART OF SELLING
from SmarterComics

by Tom Hopkins

A national bestseller, with over one million copies sold in its original version, this book is a classic for teaching the tools of selling success. Lauded by motivational icon Zig Ziglar, the author has been called "America's #1 sales trainer."

FORTUNE FAVORS THE BOLD from SmarterComics

by Franco Arda

Written by the founder of SmarterComics, this powerful little manual packs a punch. If you want to grab life by the horns but tend to drag your feet doing it, this comic is for you.

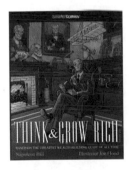

THINK & GROW RICH from SmarterComics

by Napoleon Hill

Want to learn the principles of getting rich in less than an hour? Take the illustrated advice of millionaire Andrew Carnegie, whose observations make up the heart of the best-selling classic "Think and Grow Rich." Now updated into an engaging comic book format, you can quickly glean Carnegie's wisdom from these beautifully illustrated panels.

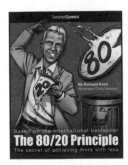

THE 80/20 PRINCIPLE from SmarterComics

by Richard Koch

Learn the time-tested secret of achieving more with less using "the 80/20 Principle." Based on the counter-intuitive fact that 80% of results flow from 20% of causes, it is the guiding principle of highly effective people and organizations.

Quiz

Please visit www.smartercomics.com/quiz for the answers and more quizzes.

Q: The spirit of Void is the spirit of:

    A. Darkness.

    B. Nothingness.

    C. Being uncaring.

Q: What is the "twofold gaze"?

    A. Sight, which is weak, and perception, which is strong.

    B. A stare that can cow an enemy or soothe a comrade.

    C. The ability to appear to be paying attention when you are not.

Q: In combat, not knowing a weapon is a fault. Equally dangerous is:

    A. Follow as many different theories of strategy as possible.

    B. Practice constantly.

    C. Work with the best teachers in the world.

Q: In order to succeed in the Way of strategy, you must:

    A. Follow as many different theories of strategy as possible.

    B. Practice constantly.

    C. Work with the best teachers in the world.

Q: Like the carpenter, the commander in battle must know:

    A. The natural rules of country and houses.

    B. How to build effective fortifications.

    C. How to work with a team of individuals with different goals and work ethics.

Q: Contrary to the movements of a large group, the movements of an individual are difficult to predict because:

A. The individual is often overlooked.

B. The individual can adapt and change his mind quickly.

C. The individual can use stealth more easily than a group.

Q: The Book of Fire is primarily concerned with conflict and fighting. The essence of the Book of Fire is that you must:

A. Train day and night in order to make quick decisions.

B. Exercise to build your strength and stamina.

C. Train with numerous weapons in order to quickly defeat the enemy.

Q: No matter the "weapon" you use, the Way of strategy is the spirit of:

A. Survival.

B. Finding inner peace.

C. Winning.

Q: When you take up the sword, you should be intent only on:

A. Parrying your opponents attacks.

B. Protecting those who are weaker than you.

C. Cutting the enemy.

Q: The sure way to win a fight is by:

A. Having a stronger force than your opponent.

B. Controlling the battle.

C. Developing better fighting techniques.

www.smartercomics.com